HOLY B

'*Holy Boys*, the second collection by 1
Ordorica, brims with lush and sensu

the page like a cumbia-tinged sunrise. Gorgeously multilingual,
stylistically varied, and resistant to centring any single narrative or
facet of identity, *Holy Boys* is a formally innovative and beautifully
meditative collection that is both dynamic and full of heart'

ALYCIA PIRMOHAMED

'Andrés N. Ordorica is a phenomenal poet, his words will lift you,
hold you, enchant you. *Holy Boys* is an exquisite and exceptional
collection, and I highly recommend you read it, treasure it
and share it'

SALENA GODDEN

'*Holy Boys* lives in the borderlands of memory, unspooling
a childhood. Spectral, melodic, quietly forceful like the sea,
these poems house oceans of dreaming and remembrance. The
multilingual poem, slipping between languages and between
different voices, gives shape to a complex family portrait, and the
formation of intimacy and longing. This is a tender and
vivid collection'

NINA MINGYA POWLES

'Poem after poem warns against the danger of forgetting, the loss
we encounter in neglecting both the beauty and difficulty of our
individual histories. Ordorica's poems look past mere survival
and fold the whole of his story into a determined and optimistic
present; "I won't blow out the candles" he promises, "instead,
I'll be the light"'

MARJORIE LOTFI

A NOTE ON THE AUTHOR

Andrés N. Ordorica is a queer Latinx writer based in Edinburgh. His debut poetry collection, *At Least This I Know*, was published in 2022, and his debut novel, *How We Named the Stars*, was published in 2024. He has been shortlisted for the Morley Lit Prize, the Mo Siewcharran Prize and the Saltire Society's Poetry Book of The Year. In 2024, he was selected as one of the *Observer*'s 10 Best Debut Novelists.

HOLY BOYS

ANDRÉS N. ORDORICA

Polygon

First published in paperback in Great Britain in 2025 by
Polygon, an imprint of Birlinn Ltd.

Birlinn Ltd
West Newington House
10 Newington Road
Edinburgh EH9 1QS

9 8 7 6 5 4 3 2 1

www.polygonbooks.co.uk

ISBN 978 1 84697 688 9
eBook ISBN 978 1 78885 729 1

British Library Cataloguing-in-Publication Data
A catalogue record for this book is available
from the British Library.

Typeset in Verdigris MVB by The Foundry, Edinburgh
Printed and bound in Great Britain by Clays Ltd, Elcograf S.p.A.

MIX
Paper | Supporting
responsible forestry
FSC® C018072

CONTENTS

Empty Words   1

I

Crescendo   7
Hurt   8
I have been dreaming   9
Red, Red, Red   10
Maricones   12
In praise of quiet boys   13
La tercera rueda   14
La tercera rueda (The third wheel)   15

II

Mirasol (what I see in Mother)   19
La Reza del Viento   20
Dream place   22
A Man of Silences   24
Pelo Negro   26
Divine Nationhood   28
Memory Map   30
Tenochtitlán   36

III

An Echo Across Time   39

The purpose that was lost   40

Heron   42

On the birthday of the World   43

Fourth of July   44

IV

Dolens annus   47

Sevenling (This is my body . . .)   48

What I know of body   49

My lover's hands   50

Why I will not get out of bed   52

I used to keep a list   53

If life were a movie   54

Gay by definition   55

V

Do you struggle with homosexuality?   59

Good Friday   60

If I could pray the gay away   62

Our bodies   63

When the wild calls   64

In the Woods   65

The river turns into a waterfall   66

VI

Seven feathers   71

Norway (our way)   72

Cuarenta y una mariposas monarcas

bailan debajo una lluvia de verano   74

Forty-one monarch butterflies   76

dancing in a summer shower   76

queer men.   77

In the name of the Joto, Mariposa y Maricón   78

Here There Everywhere   80

We shall gather   82

VII

Long distance   87

Dating from across an ocean   88

We do not change   89

My husband the atheist   90

The bells   92

Tagus   93

A Pile of Green Peas   94

Balmedie   96

Harr Rising   97

Glossary / Glosario   99

Acknowledgements   100

For Kevin

What I give you, give me,
and break me free.

from 'By The Fire' by Edwin Morgan

EMPTY WORDS

after Zaffar Kunial

Volver, Volver, or a
doubled returning – I hear not
'Chente' but Papá – *to where I ask?*

*

Each Sunday the Father commanded:
'Go in Peace to Love and Serve' –
outside finches always greeted us.

*

In Latin America some use Vosotros –
opposite of *We* – a collective *You*,
but all I hear in *vos* is *voz*.

*

Papá always said, 'If you don't believe,
you don't receive.' And did that mean
gifts, Christ or love – synonyms?

*

My mother's land is desert and sand:
Chihuahua like *agua*, but water
is a scarce word for a dry mouth.

*

I was born between the border of
two silent places – my mother's dreaming;
my father's prayers.

*

Under April sun, I play with
dandelions all fluff no roar;
my father shouts: *ball, ball, ball!*

*

In baseball, we run diamonds,
and I wonder if I'll ever shine
as bright as a ruby; July 4th, the sun.

*

It's baseball or *beisbol* not *besos*
which my father always gives me;
masculinity isn't the opposite of love.

*

To hear me as I should, I say:
Andrés like undress – which is
to bare myself in a foreign tongue.

*

My mom slips all her tongues in one:
ese pendejo, ese cabrón, ese pinche troublemaker . . .
I could write a thousand essays on *that, that, that*.

*

My father is twice removed
American by way of Jalisco by way of Zacatecas –
a history more storied than we knew.

*

I was the middle child – an 'A' in
the middle of two Ss – my siblings'
two Ss propagated from our parentS:

*

Salvador, Sonia, Salvador,
Andrés, Selyssa; decades later
a surprise 'E': Enrique.

*

Prayer is not the words,
but receiving none and still believing –
in poetry, this is allusion.

*

The crack of hide against wood;
the crowd is ROARing, and I am
enveloped in that sea of dandelions.

I

CRESCENDO

at the peak of a wave
just before it comes crashing down
is where i feel belonging

before the tide can push me out
or the tide can drag me in
before i wash away the tired shore

HURT

Noun
1. the room felt cold
like being forgotten

2. and he felt empty and lost
(see: *vacant*; *breakable*)

'This boy is far too soft.'

Adjective
Memories at the centre
of pitch darkness: black plum

'The light is opposite –
a vortex destroying my delicate body.'

Verb
Disguised as love.
(see: *look after*; *raise*; *nurture*)

'Hurt is not a home.'

of the boy I was at seven / at twelve / at fifteen / the one who made
himself small enough to pass through the eye of a needle / camel
bent in prayer / origami crane's sharp folds / steaming tortilla
fresh off the comal / wrapped tightly and under duress / the fear
that poisoned his body / anxiety leaking into his fragile heart /
all that pain he hid away in broom closets and chests of drawers
/ where did it go? / is it still out there? / one small shift will cause
seismic plates to collide / those tidal waves will crash / the hurt
I'll have to reckon with / debris left upon the shore / queer joy
can only plaster over so much / forgetting is not survival / love is
love is not freedom / eventually I'll wake and have to face what
my dreams are telling me / a little boy wants answers / a little boy
has questions / you see a little boy is out there.

RED, RED, RED

When I was a boy,
I wanted to be drawn
in Crayola fire-engine red,
the brightest colour of a flame.

When I was a boy,
I wanted to be Clifford;
I wanted to be the Chicago Bulls;
I wanted to be a red convertible:
the one all the other boys wanted.
Oh, how I wanted them to covet me.

I wanted to be rouged cheeks.
I wanted to paint my lips in Revlon.
Just like mom.

I wanted to be the red of anger.
I wanted to be a lady in red.
I wanted to bleed red:

drip

       drip

              drip.

When I was a boy,
I wanted nothing more
than to be autumn's final leaf:

strong enough to stop October
from buckling to winter,
all its death to come.

MARICONES

Mijo, don't play with that, she says.
And so, Araceli's muñequita is taken yet again from me.
Really, Rogelia, he shouldn't be playing with his sister's toys.
Is this a 'rule rule' or just one of Abuela's? I ask myself.
Can't you see how all the other boys laugh at you?
Oh, I say, pushing down my contempt for that bruja vieja.
Now, now, my mother tuts as she sweeps in.
Enough fighting. Mijo, go afuera to play with your primos.
She quickly pushes me out into another lonesome afternoon.

IN PRAISE OF QUIET BOYS

who house oceans inside them
greek fire burning atop emerald water

whose hearts pulse in anger
wild pain that could bring cities
down in one fell swoop

no body spared

in praise of quiet boys
who've broken so many noses open
clenched fists never swung

who in their mind
always have a perfect comeback
boys more than their darkness storming

these boys are siphons of masculinity
the kind you'll never find on streets

these boys are more than their quietude
the kind that speaks volumes

hand in form of mouth

LA TERCERA RUEDA

La luna me dijo
que no pudo
dormir sin
la compañía
del sol.

Y el sol
me dijo que
no quiere existir
sin la compañía
de la luna.

Pero nadie
me preguntó como
yo quiero vivir.

LA TERCERA RUEDA (THE THIRD WHEEL)

The Poet's Translation

The moon said
it could not
sleep
without
the sun.

The sun
told me
it did not
exist
without
the moon.

But neither
asked me how
I wanted to live.

II

MIRASOL (WHAT I SEE IN MOTHER)

When I think of my mother
she is that shade of ochre
as summer slips away.

She is like warmth slowly
dipping along an equinox
warning winter is near.

What was sown deep
tilled in frosted earth
my mother will guard.

In autumn's ripe reflection
I sense this shift in season
how time will pause.

So, we might begin to take stock.
So, we might begin to prepare
for a long winter's sleep.

But when spring comes,
my mother will sunflower;
me blossoming brightly by her side.

LA REZA DEL VIENTO

In the tussle of a windstorm,
I rush to catch tus palabras
the ones you gave me,
in our shared multi tongues.

In the autumn lluvia,
I bathe myself lentamente
in the silent 'h' and rolling 'r'
of *hermoso*, the name for me:
your handsome prince.

Under afternoon sky,
I bask in slivered luz y heat
las nubes bailan arriba.
El viento how it sings for us –
just listen for a minute!

querido

      hermoso

           querido

                hermoso

I feel you in my spirit, mi alma,
te lo juro, I sense you in the trees.
I am five again, I am ten, twenty:
Te quiero mucho mi niño hermoso.

I love you too, mi rey. Oh, sweet man.
Duerme bien y descansa un rato.

We will see each other again,
lo prometo, soon enough:

Si Dios quiere,
        mi niño hermoso,
                Si Dios quiere.

In the tussle of a windstorm,
I stand under October skies
breathing in all your dying words.

DREAM PLACE

From your plastic patio chair, you nod along to the lyrics, this story, all of which I've heard before:

Cazadores on the mesa, a white linen mantel, your wedding day. Everyone you love in attendance.

Truth is I wasn't there, but I imagine someone pours out the añejo, another cuts the lime, you will make a speech.

This will be the last time you ever speak in public, silent man, but still, you do.

People laugh, the bride cries, you feel a sense of pride.

You salt the space between index and thumb. Two modest wedding bands glimmer in the light, hers and yours, honey liquid shots in hand.

¡Arriba, abajo, al centro, pa' dentro!

It stings as it goes down, but you welcome its warmth.

People clap as the band starts up.

You call to her like a song playing in some lonesome cantina.

To complete this ceremony, I will lay out her lipstick, silver framed photo, *a real María Félix*, my grandmother.

Her ofrenda before us – I will add a glass bowl of her favourite strawberry candies wrapped in shiny Christmas colours. Dollar-store best.

We should pray, I'll say. More songs will play from the radio, a sepia tinged México more yours than mine. You will tell me about the first time you heard this song.

I will half listen to your slurred speech, electing to commence prayers as you monologue, fearing the wick will blow out.

Raising my hand like your son taught me: *En el nombre del Padre, y del Hijo, y del Espíritu Santo.*

I will look to you, but you will not be following along. Instead, you are singing a love song from a time gone by.

I will let the candles burn themselves out. I will walk you to your room, guiding you.

There, we will say prayers together as you return to where you long to be.

It has been light years since and only one half of you remains, but still, your mind returns.

A MAN OF SILENCES

My grandfather sits quietly
alone in a pew unsure if
morning mass has begun.

My grandfather sits quietly
in a living room of language
and laughter not his own.

My grandfather sits quietly
in an outside house he built
so that he might cry softly

long into midnight.

My grandfather in sadness
at my dying grandmother's bedside,
sarcoma's alchemy at work.

My grandfather lost in thought
as I am kneeling by his side,
trying to surface a perfect phrase

wrestling our forgotten tongue.

Abuelo, a man of silences,
listens to his grandson
finally say: *I love you*

in every language
we (n)ever shared.

PELO NEGRO

He cuts my hair, thick
blackness the colour of petrol
density of a slumbering panther
in the shadow of its dreaming.

He asks me, *Where are you from?*
and maybe it isn't loaded
but maybe it always is
because to be from somewhere
is to *not be* from here.

I think of Soledad, mi bisabuela,
her white hair long as memory
plaited into a flowing border
down the column of her back.

I think of empires and revolutions,
all that sacred knowledge
of those original people
their lost languages – how even
Mother's tongue is lost to me.

With each clip of hair,
the ground pools to black;
the strands wrap themselves
around me.

'So, where are you from?'

Smiling, I counter back.

'How long you got?'

As I lay claim to each place,
name, epoch, gathering
every strand.

No longer afraid,
no longer uncertain
of where roots begin.

DIVINE NATIONHOOD

'I thank God, I was born a Mexican.'
                                        My mother

Gracias a Dios,
I was born a Mexican
under el Bajo Sexto moon
in the eye of a cumbia-
tinged sunrise.

Thanks be to God
que nací con una serpiente
en mi boca
as the eagle soared high
among the Gods.

That I was raised
on el ritmo
del Jarabe Tapatío
that my heart follows
its beat, I thank God.

¡Gracias a Dios!
Like really
thanks be to Them!

What divine grace
to be born a Mexican
to feel like a sun

with all its rays
fierce luminosity
brightly burning.

MEMORY MAP

after Jennifer Wong's 'Mountain City'

i.

She cuts patterns from
leather unfurled like maps
of where her grandchildren
will go to find themselves.

Metal gliding along
eggshell blue, rich taupe,
the height of fifties' fashion
each side of an imagined border.

He offers her forever,
his promise the coordinates
of a prosperous place
that does not yet exist.

She weighs her decision
like cow's hide on market day
before relenting
to a life of dreaming
which is not her own.

ii.

I fell asleep after hours spent
circling back on a history
that was all red dirt,
dried tumbleweed

fence of stubborn nopales,
tuna rosa creciendo.
The lazy burro
posted to his fence.

I awoke to skin
Colorado-red and hot,
my hair the black
of death. I was scared

by the reflection
in a bathroom mirror.
My body read
like an epic poem, unearthing
our bloodied legacy.

iii.

Scorched grass
burning skin as he slides
from base to base;
his whooping watchful fans.

Bleachers sticky with beer
and sunflower shells.
Wooden bat hitting leather
ball; that thudding sound

reverberates decades on
as his youngest stands
behind the mound,
dreaming of what he'll do

when autumn comes
and he will no longer
pretend to love
his father's favourite
season.

iv.

Cumbias play from speakers
bought on discount
in a house 13,000 miles
from where her history

begins. She dilutes Clorox
in two-thirds water, mixes
as Selena's dulcet voice
rouses three sleeping kids.

Saturday morning means
together they'll strip
the walls of their weekly
dirt and memory.

Dancing like washing
machines, as she sings
along to a legend,
that once forbidden love.

v.

We walk along wide
avenidas under jacaranda
blossoming, and cicadas
calling out to greet us.

You tell me how you
adore the feeling of skin
warm like a pink concha
fresh from the oven,

and all I want is to hold
you close enough
to smell the cinnamon
and orange blossom

of your hair, dunk you
in hot café and show
you how this is the most
me you've ever known.

How this brown, ochre
red, copper, leather me,
finally, for once,
is whole.

vi.

He is driving me
around his hometown.
The one he once found
from coordinates

written on a second-hand
map. I roll a window
down to feel the wind
rustling hair on my forearm.

He points, one after
another, all the iron gates
he fashioned to protect
this town's families.

I turn to him and take
in his hands, mottled
and thick from daily
labour, and all I want

is to share with him
how he taught me
to fashion memory
like hot ore: *Do you
know poetry is also iron?*

TENOCHTITLÁN

I stood there
above waking orange
sinking into
an ancient valley

I listened in the gloam
of bustling dawn
as denizens and trucks
moved about their days

I closed my eyes to see
stone aqueducts, pyramids
erected all around me
in this former Tenochtitlán

Millennia ago:
Did the sun rise in such copper splendour?
Did cardenalitos call out across the valley?
Was man allowed to stop and dream?

III

AN ECHO ACROSS TIME

In this city, you'll find history
stuffed inside its gutters,
carved into its brickwork.

If you listen, you'll hear
its memories humming
above rain-slicked cobble,
lapping in waves against the Forth.

Such mellifluous poetry and song;
tales written into banisters,
laments sung under street lamp,
how they mirror the times.

Dancing across centuries,
the past playing on my mind,
remember to heed its warning:

there's a reason history
echoes across time.

THE PURPOSE THAT WAS LOST

I forgot my house plant
or should I say desk plant?

As I packed up my keyboard
and my mouse,
I thought of cat-like ambition,
another thing I didn't know.
I thought of the sloth
unsure how fast it moves.

the gentle whipped nothingness
to show for a day.

On the last day in my office,
I quietly left my desk;
I walked into a cubicle
cried – had a panic attack.

drifting towards a whirlpool,
towards a freedom that scared me.

To be purposefully
un-purposeful
would be to betray
my immigrant blood.

I dreamt of a shark
swimming in cold waters
– *alone and fierce.*

I walked through quiet,
abandoned streets
unsure if the tide was leading.

I forgot my map
swimming towards
a nothingness,
totally aware of
the lack of purpose
that awaits . . .

that would wash over me
in never-ending
solitude.

HERON

Curlicues of slurred words   roll off my tongue
as speckled thoughts pour out   into the dark of night

    silence otherwise is in abundance
        as we traverse open meadow:

    I stop mid-thought,
    fracture verb and noun,
    to give space
    to a majestic
    ethereal bird.

    [Reader, I am drunk, but I swear to God,
        in the silence of a cold March evening,
        in the middle of a city park,
            a heron stands in all her glory,
            and I have nothing left to say.]

ON THE BIRTHDAY OF THE WORLD

after Marge Piercy

I'll leave behind
the thumbing scroll of blue light

I'll walk into a forest bath
pause in the presence of trees
look skyward

I'll shake off doubt
as the clocks ring in change
I'll ask the moon's advice

In a throng of revellers,
I'll open my arms to love
remembering we can and will

I'll map stars, hold hope
like Ursa Minor and Ursa Major,
I'll bear hug a stranger

I won't blow out the candles
instead, I'll be the light

FOURTH OF JULY
after Barbara Crooker

If I could travel at the speed of light / I would burn a thousand
sparklers / I would write each letter / send it to the past so my
past self (read: younger self) could see / could read each letter
illuminating in the dark / a thousand times over: I / L / O /
these messages from light years ahead: V / E / . . . I never wrote
them for me / this message spelled in golden streaks will show
you / yes / Y / O/ U / how far we'll go / just how far light travels.

IV

DOLENS ANNUS

This year, I came to understand
the body can carry much more pain
than we tend to give it credit for

SEVENLING (THIS IS MY BODY . . .)

This is my body, let me introduce it:
the greeting acid reflux, storied chin + eyebrow cut
all which follow me like regret.

There are things it doesn't show
like how I cry in bathrooms, masturbate late
afternoon, scream into the gloaming.

In the mirror is a boy searching for the answer.

WHAT I KNOW OF BODY

'I took what there was –
or allowed what there was to take me . . .'

JAMES BALDWIN, *Another Country*

My body is container / holding men
in each / vessel of opportunity
to capture what of them I liked the most

My body is page / lines of men
are written on skin / filled with
honest frank reviews / mood killer

My body is billboard / luring men
with promised acts / opening wide
the line is round the block / cock tease

My body is pilot light / waiting for spark
our bed in need of warmth / I'll burn him
first / unless he snuffs my flame

MY LOVER'S HANDS

after Edwin Morgan's 'Pilate at Fortingall'

I am more mindful now of my lover's body
and the cautious way it takes up [   ]
or gives [   ], so not to die, so to live.

How he washes his hands, and watches his
hands, and washes his hands, and watches
his hands, and washes his hands, and watch.

How he jumps two steps forward, three to the
side so he might extend his life, this is
the new world order: what it is not to die.

I am more mindful of how I cry when
I close the door, or when I have a wank,
or when I think this could go on for ever.

I am more mindful of how my lover's body
could be a carrier for this viral thing
that is invisibly killing everyone around us.

So, he washes his hands, and watches his
hands, and washes his hands, and watches
his hands, but doesn't use his hands to touch.

He doesn't touch my body like he used to
touch my body, like nobody touches any
body any more, nobody touches me any more.

And whenever I wash my hands, or try to
hold hands, or try to throw hands, or try
to fold my hands, I cannot get them to pray.

It makes no sense, surely, we are mad for
thinking we can stand to not hold hands
the rest of our godforsaken lives.

Each day, I wake up naked and hopeful
that today might be the day, his hands hold
mine, that today might be the day. We can.

WHY I WILL NOT GET OUT OF BED

after James Tate

My skin sheds
like a morning glory:
I only open at dawn

in secret places. I will
learn to keep inside
the nectar you long

to sup each morning
while mourning
what we once had.

In winter I will lay
dormant under frosted
earth – I will be a bird,
the bee, Mother Nature.

Spring will call
to me. I won't answer
as eagerly as I did
in my youth.

of all the men I slept with: names and dates. Because I feared
what forgetting might say of me. I used it for archival purposes,
mapping out ill decisions and summer flings, man to man,
from bed to bed (or alleyways, sometimes cars). I kept that list
because I feared reprisal, or more so, I feared judgement, which
might come if I could not name each body that had been in my
body. I slut-shamed myself, walked my shame back home in
the morning as if it were a cross I had to carry, but the thing is
I liked it: all that sex. Man on man, man in man, mano y mano,
all their hands all over my body. Their salty lips, my scratched
hips, ripped jeans, from prostrating on bended knees. I loved
knowing my body could do all that (did all that), but I lost that
list some time ago, and so, I lost that version of me, the man I
was becoming as each letter curled itself from one name into
the next, serif spilling over from one bed into the last.

IF LIFE WERE A MOVIE

the person who stars as me
would be five inches taller
with biceps ten inches wider

His hair would be obsidian black
his eyes speckled in fool's gold
he would take the frame
and turn the focus on himself

If life were a movie
someone would feed me words
and I'd happily play along

GAY BY DEFINITION

Hit them with the old razzle dazzle;
sink your teeth into their lush peach.
Recreate the watery cancer star sign
as the moon pulls you towards desire.

Trade fairy tales for gritty war stories
of torn jeans, skinned knees, broken jaws –
I mean a fairy's tale is one of survival
and survival is a tea best served hot.

If they yell out 'faggot', turn right round,
high kick them in the throat, death drop
onto their face so they suffocate from
all your ass, death by cake, 'Let them eat it.'

V

DO YOU STRUGGLE WITH HOMOSEXUALITY?

Asked the pastor.
'No,' I said.
He nodded slowly.
I stared him down,
and that was that.

GOOD FRIDAY

The curtain was pulled back
and at my feet stood the Holy Mother
and Mary Magdalene – two bored girls
the year above me. It was too late.

Neither woman could protect me.
Neither woman could stop the madness.
Neither cared about the pain I held.

For seven minutes, in front of my entire
confirmation class, I stayed standing,
strung up on a large cross, naked to the waist.

How diligently I kept my eyes shut
even when the soldiers, three burly boys
from school, lifted me down, a broken body
caressed by their sinewy arms – whiff of musk and longing.

Oh, how they crucified me, just like they did our Lord,
then how they wrapped me in virgin muslin.
I didn't breathe a single breath – *I swear to you.*
With eyes held shut I let them bury me in the tomb.

If only the crowd knew the truth of who I was . . .
they'd have crucified me a thousand times over;
they'd have lanced me each with their judgements;
they'd have stoned me in verse and dogma and hellfire.

Until all my many coloured lights, all my hidden desires
poured out of me and stained what was once white and pure–
red violent blood and blue silent tears shed upon the rock.

IF I COULD PRAY THE GAY AWAY

... I would not I would not I would not I would not I would not
I would not I would not I would not I would not I would not I
would not I would not I would not I would not I would not I
would not I would not I would not I would not I would not I
would not I would not I would not I would not I would not I
would not I would not I would not I would not I would not I
would not I would not I would not I would not I would not I
would not I would not I would not I would not I would not I
would not I would not I would not I would not I would not I
would not I would not I would not I would not I would not I
would not I would not I would not I would not I would not I
would not I would not I would not I would not I would not I
would not I would not I would not I would not I would not I
would not I would not I would not I would not I would not I
would not I would not I would not I would not I would not I
would not I would not I would not I would not I would not I
would not I would not I would not ...

OUR BODIES

Our bodies are spring garden
Our bodies are dormant seedlings
Our bodies are the tower of Babel
Our bodies are Father, Son and Holy Ghost
Our bodies are vestigial anecdote, ancestral secret
Our bodies are golden ochre crunch of autumn
Our bodies are grey, purple black of winter
Our bodies are the possibility of years unfolding
Our bodies are turquoise clarity of a summer baptism
Our bodies are passed on to the next inheritor

WHEN THE WILD CALLS

quiet on the Sabbath morning
soft on a still winter's eve
moonlit prayers surrendered
resilient when death no longer tugs

enigma which is unfamiliar to itself
echoes in the darkness of our minds
maudlin as dust dances in the light
knowingness swelling above clear water

peaceful on the splintered harbour's edge
hopeful on the cusp of autumn's dawn
chaos in shrouds of clouded anger
we bridge the chasm of ancestral trauma

names we will never truly understand
names we have no language for

when we hear them, we will answer
when the wild calls to us, we will know

IN THE WOODS

after Tishani Doshi

They are coming out of the woods like leaves blowing in the wind. Only to be pushed further out across the land. In droves, they are singing loudly. Exuberant, fearsome even. These former quiet sprites, invisible not from want but survival. If only to see another day. But now they cloak themselves in every spool of thread, dressed in every type of cloth. Some are proud in the single space they occupy. Others still are ever-changing, and, still, others are ciphers, coded solely to make sense to kindred spirits in the know. There in the forest live all the clues to their existence. How for millennia, they have always walked the earth. This we know. They have been sending smoke signals from one generation to the next until finally saying *no more.* In the face of great fear, in the face of great violence, it is braver to leave the safety of the trees, if only to see the light, to feel the sun. If only to fight back. Yes, they are coming out of the woods. They are running out of the woods. They are dancing out of the woods. We are howling in the wind. Likes trees, we shake. Like trees, we stand. In the woods, where we have always been.

THE RIVER TURNS INTO A WATERFALL

the beavers
are making den
on the edge
where the river

      turns
      into
      a waterfall

      at the place
      their den

      becomes
      a dam

a beaver den (or lodge)
is a seasonal home
entered through water

         free from predators
         tucked away neatly
         hidden in the forest

     i am a beaver
        edging his way
           towards
           the lodge

under murky water
tall, yellowed reeds
       cattails swaying
      i find them

my fellow beavers
they ask me

            will you help today
            will you make den
            with us?

aye my friends
today
i will make a den
to pass the winter in

and when
spring comes
          i will swim back
          to the surface
      breathe in
      the flowery air

VI

SEVEN FEATHERS

I swam out to the cove
as evening waned

      letting water do the work
      I focused on the sky

           rock face framed for me
           night-time firmament

               seven feathers floated by

           sensing time unfolding
           understanding nature's change

      I was ready to ascend
      grow wings

made of seven feathers
floating in the wind

NORWAY (OUR WAY)

Lately, my siblings and I have been sending text messages like radar signals across the Atlantic. Messages by four siblings who let life get in the way because sometimes that is the way, but there is always time to change direction – always time to redirect. My siblings and I have been using group chats like lighthouses warning ships at sea of the breaking waves crashing upon the tired shores of adulthood and marriage and studying and kids and life without kids and loneliness in a life surrounded by others surrounded by all that noise trying to catch a break. Like one day I am running across fields of gorse in grey heat but how bright the yellow lights my way. I pause and take a photo – lately I have been taking photos like an archivist fighting the loneliness rolling in like haar across the Forth – I tell them what is in the photo so they can know my life, so they might know me more after we have lost our way, and let distance grow unwieldy along the way. I tell them in the corner is the North Sea – *You see there in grey-blue. If you followed its currents, you'd sail all the way to Norway!* – I tell them this because I want them to know my life. I want my life to be their life, to be our lives once again. Because they have known me longer than any other people in this world have known me and I don't want to lose that. I don't want to shut myself out any more from being known in that way. I no longer want to be enigma to them. These three that share my blood, my ancestry, my memories of a lonely life surrounded by three others, surrounded by all that I thought made me different, too different, for them to want to know me, to see me as I was, as I am. Three bright lights, my radar signals, my people bonded by life. I send the picture in a text message, and I hope it says to them: *Come to me along the currents across the sea. I am waiting. I will always be waiting.* I pray it reads loudly: *I am here for you. We will find our way back to each other. We will land on the shores of life and breathe in salted air. We will make up for lost time.* Pull back the haar and let all that bright yellow light pour out – *I have missed you!*

CUARENTA Y UNA MARIPOSAS MONARCAS
BAILAN DEBAJO UNA LLUVIA DE VERANO

(a migration translation)

```
\\\\\    \\\\\    \\\\\    \\\\\    \\\\\    \\\\\    \\\\\    \\\\\
\\\\\    \\\\\    \\\\\    \\\\\    \\\\\    \\\\\    \\\\\    \\\\\
\\\\\    \\\\\    \\\\\    \\\\\    \\\\\    \\\\\    \\\\\    \\\\\
\\\\\    \\\\\    \\\\\    \\\\\    \\\\\    \\\\\    \\\\\    \\\\\
\\\\\    \\\\\    \\\\\    \\\\\    \\\\\    \\\\\    \\\\\    \\\\\
\\\\\    \\\\\    \\\\\    \\\\\    \\\\\    \\\\\    \\\\\    \\\\\
\\\\\    \\\\\    \\\\\    \\\\\    \\\\\    \\\\\    \\\\\    \\\\\
\\\\\    \\\\\    \\\\\    \\\\\    \\\\\    \\\\\    \\\\\    \\\\\
```

```
          >!< >!<>!< >!<
          >!< >!< >!< >!<
>!< >!< >!< >!<
>!< >!< >!< >!<
              >!< >!< >!< >!<
              >!< >!< >!< >!<
              >!< >!< >!< >!<
>!< >!<              >!<>!<
     >!< >!<              >!< >!<
          >!< >!<
          >!< >!<
              >!<
```

```
\\\\\    \\\\\    \\\\\    \\\\\    \\\\\    \\\\\    \\\\\    \\\\\
\\\\\    \\\\\    \\\\\    \\\\\    \\\\\    \\\\\    \\\\\    \\\\\
\\\\\    \\\\\    \\\\\    \\\\\    \\\\\    \\\\\    \\\\\    \\\\\
\\\\\    \\\\\    \\\\\    \\\\\    \\\\\    \\\\\    \\\\\    \\\\\
```

```
\\\\    \\\\    \\\\    \\\\    \\\\    \\\\    \\\\    \\\\
\\\\    \\\\    \\\\    \\\\    \\\\    \\\\    \\\\    \\\\
\\\\    \\\\    \\\\    \\\\    \\\\    \\\\    \\\\    \\\\
\\\\    \\\\    \\\\    \\\\    \\\\    \\\\    \\\\    \\\\
```

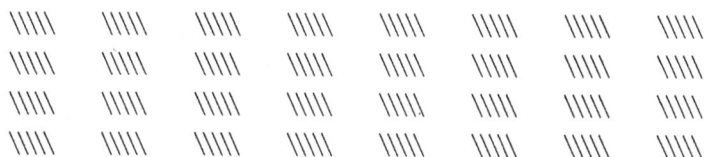

¡Y las mariposas vuelan y regresan a un paraíso de flores y miel! Están a salvo de todo el odio del mundo.

FORTY-ONE MONARCH BUTTERFLIES
DANCING IN A SUMMER SHOWER

(una poema sin fronteras)

```
/////    /////    /////    /////    /////    /////    /////    /////
/////    /////    /////    /////    /////    /////    /////    /////
/////    /////    /////    /////    /////    /////    /////    /////
/////    /////    /////    /////    /////    /////    /////    /////
/////    /////    /////    /////    /////    /////    /////    /////
/////    /////    /////    /////    /////    /////    /////    /////
/////    /////    /////    /////    /////    /////    /////    /////
/////    /////    /////    /////    /////    /////    /////    /////
/////    /////    /////    /////    /////    /////    /////    /////
```

```
         >¡< >¡<         >¡< >¡<
         >¡< >¡<         >¡< >¡<
>¡< >¡<          >¡< >¡<
>¡< >¡<          >¡< >¡<
                 >¡< >¡<         >¡< >¡<
                 >¡< >¡<         >¡< >¡<
                 >¡< >¡<         >¡< >¡<
>¡< >¡<          >¡< >¡<
                 >¡< >¡<         >¡< >¡<
                 >¡< >¡<
                 >¡< >¡<
                          >¡<
```

```
/////    /////    /////    /////    /////    /////    /////    /////
/////    /////    /////    /////    /////    /////    /////    /////
/////    /////    /////    /////    /////    /////    /////    /////
```

```
/////    /////    /////    /////    /////    /////    /////    /////
/////    /////    /////    /////    /////    /////    /////    /////
/////    /////    /////    /////    /////    /////    /////    /////
/////    /////    /////    /////    /////    /////    /////    /////
/////    /////    /////    /////    /////    /////    /////    /////
/////    /////    /////    /////    /////    /////    /////    /////
```

Mariposa (Spanish for 'Butterfly') is often used as a homophobic slur against queer men.

IN THE NAME OF THE JOTO, MARIPOSA Y MARICÓN

I offer this prayer up in the name of the Joto, limp-wristed Mariposa, y irreverent Maricón. The ones who saw bravado like the Spanish Inquisition –

a machismo that could smell testosterone death dropping off the scale, ready to kill us.

I bear witness to the little boys swaying hips like Whirlpool washing machines while dreaming in sequence: leotard, red lipstick, diamanté-encrusted bustier.

Imagining us as our own leyendas, madre divina, anything for Selena (anything for us).

My incantation of cumbias and merengues will summon memories of watching our parents dance and studying, not our fathers, but our mothers who art in heaven –

longing to be held in that way, beautiful and vulnerable, spotlit and telenovela pretty.

I lift my hands up blessing this Eucharist, the altar before us – divining the DJ to play one more Paulina, Thalía, Shakira canción por que under our abuela's eyes we are safe:

'Ay, hijo. ¡Cálmate! And leave him alone. He's just having a little fun.'

As we shake our bidi bidi bom bom while watching the clock because when the clock strikes one then we're done and back to little boys we go.

So, worship with me in this sacred moment, safe in this communion – let the música y ritmo protegerte my little apostles, praise the joyful colour, luminous freedom as you repeat after me:

We are Holy Faggots, santos maricones, we are happy little boys having a little fun.

We are staking claim in who we really are: holy, holy, holy boys.

We are beautiful, *telenovela pretty* – we are our own leyendas.

We are mariposas unfurling from our crisálidas.

We are Holy, Holy, Holy.

We are whole.

Amén.

HERE THERE EVERYWHERE

For the elders we never got to meet

You longed to see the world
in all your glory
like morning glory,
roots buried deep in earth.

You said, *I will get there.*
You said, *I will reach
that dream place.*

Be happy, I will be happy,
you said like prayer.

I sometimes wonder
what our bond
would be like – its weight?

If I told you,
I, too, am looking at maps
to find happiness as place.

If I told you,
your name I bear,
all of its letters, full of power.

I will carry you (una promesa)
for ever across this earth.

I will plant you
in each new place.
Show you the world
is so much more than hate.

WE SHALL GATHER

after Juan Felipe Herrera

to breathe all the way in blessing

we shall gather on the hillside
steadied by gorse and grass

we will meet night above sea
birdsong playing to infinite stars

to breathe all the way in blessing

we will vibrate under an autumnal moon
around fire singing hymns to our past

we will howl with each other in delight
ocelot and coyote calling in the night

in the hands of love

when the rain pours down light and soft
don't forget to dance joyous in gratitude

welcome your ancestors, invite brethren
around to where this gathering meets

in the hands of love

when wind rises, remember to throw
your seedlings out towards the horizon

let the currents raise them skyward
let them be carried far, left to flourish

to breathe all the way in blessing

we will keep moving as the sun awakens
to where the hill bleeds into seaside

there we will wade with each other
basking in daybreak, bathing in salt pools

let us gather in a flourishing way

as we dive into bright rushing sea-foam
in a place, where we will paddle freely,
where we will breathe the air and swim all day

VII

LONG DISTANCE

There was a box in which I stored
all the letters of a lifetime

One day we will read them together
to remember what we overcame

DATING FROM ACROSS AN OCEAN

Gilda (1946)

A Place in the Sun (1951)

Gentlemen Prefer Blondes (1953)

Giant (1956)

Rebel Without a Cause (1955)

The Glass Menagerie (1950)

Love Story (1944)

Sweet Bird of Youth (1962)

Lolita (1962)

Le Mépris (1963)

Cover Girl (1944)

Some Like It Hot (1959)

Cyrano de Bergerac (1950)

Girl from Rio (1939)

WE DO NOT CHANGE

Feet shuffling on parquet floors in our first home in Kilmainham on that green isle, jewel of the Atlantic. Humming along to Céline – 'On Ne Change Pas' – pouring gin in tall crystal tumblers not our own, woozy from rented bubbles. Your company and this makeshift dance floor a tonic from that outside world. We toast glasses to all the days we will have together, to all this love we will grow. Love is the last thing I plan to do on this earth. Polishing our floors with white socked feet, dancing in the autumn light. I think to myself how we will not change or alter this gift we have. *On ne change pas.* Sing with me my love. *On ne change pas.* How true these words feel as you dance with me a little while longer in what light remains. How when we were younger, we danced and danced and danced into the rush of a new type of love. Here we are now. Years later, just the two of us, and still so much life to live.

MY HUSBAND THE ATHEIST

I will love you until the end of time
                    I know no other way to say for ever

Because our time only lasts for as long
                    on this earth we are together

Before being met by our eternal sleep
                    when you will begin to decompose

As bacterium break you down
                    this body I promised to love always

While I'll await the second coming
                    mourning you as angels lift me up

To where I will go to everlasting life
                    while you fold back into dark cold earth

You see we don't have to believe
                    in life after death, in life after our love

In order to agree we loved eternally
                    for ever, together, until the end of time

So, with whatever time we have together
                    for however long our for ever might be

I promise to be yours always and completely
                    and if never we meet in my second life

I'm glad we shared this lifetime
                    for whatever time, for however long

THE BELLS

We listened to seven bells
ringing above seven hills.

The lights flickered from ancient rooms
fado bellowing from mournful throats.

We questioned if it was our pain
sustaining these stories on the page.

The ones we had yet to write
but could hear vibrating within.

TAGUS

A road shadowed in fog
lulls me into a stupor of memories.

We have learnt to move slowly,
shifting to the continental fashion,
gazing across Lisbon's placid bay.

Half the city is azure
the other a hazy, grey Turner painting
and you, crystalline, somewhere running down below.

If I could bottle every painted tile of this city
to feed you in the dark of February's ire,
I'd scour the streets for all its ancient glass.

I would fill vessel after vessel with pigment,
mix in the dust of slippery rain slicked calçada,
snap the corks shut tight, save for a dreich day.

I'd then go out to find you
only to bring you high upon the seven hills
and feed you every memory I have
of that mighty river.

A PILE OF GREEN PEAS

after Tomás Q. Morín

What always strikes me is the green, green peas
piled together on the table – envious pea shoot
leafy lucky shamrock growing greens.

I took a photo of you later, arms spread widely.
Your smile just as open as the green lawns
which surround that gallery on the hill.

How verdant it all was the last time we saw it,
the painting I mean – my favourite colour.
The Poet and that Painter share a holy root:

'Victory of the People'.
Nicholson took inspiration from Velázquez, Golden Boy
of Seville, whose king took so much from my people.

How Nicholson captured light continues to play on my mind.
The glinting bowl, those majestic green peas, all fighting
against an encroaching shadow – lustrous somehow.

I imagine scooping up the pile, washing them
under a cold tap, patting dry, so that I might sauté them
in a little olive oil and soy sauce to serve to you.

I'd feed you from a pewter quaich adorned with rubies
atop the green grassy sun-drenched knoll. Over wine,
we'd talk of going to Velázquez's Seville, chasing the light.

I have to say that aging scares me, which is a non sequitur,
but I've known you for nearly half my life. One day
most of who we know will no longer be here – faded to time.

What will we be like at eighty? Will you still cling to me
as you fall asleep? Like now, at dawn, will you greet me with a coffee?
Will you remember green? I hope that painting still exists.

This is a round about way in twelve stanzas to say, I love you.
Like those peas, I want to etch in your mind for eternity,
never to be forgotten: lustrous, lustful, for ever in love.

We met at the dawning of our twenties.
Fresh as the white linen of Nicholson's still life.
Unblemished, ready for whatever life would bring.

One day soon, let's make our way to that side of town,
Let's walk those quiet gallery halls, holding each other
closely, as we bask in the soft slivering silver light.

BALMEDIE

The sea-grass stands
at attention like porcupine quills
or a conductor's baton.
A symphony of crashing waves
crescendo just beyond the hillocks

Mid-morning light
catches in the diamond droplets
hanging from spiders' webs.
The sandy muddy pathways
paw-print marked before us.

Sand almost white.
A blank canvas for yellowing
sea-foam washed upon the shore
as wains run up and down,
their laughter a roaring chorus.

My eyes drawn
to verdant driftwood
no longer than a hand,
its smooth bark like green tides
or swaying sea-grass in the wind.

I'll wrap it in a tired cloth,
to remind me of this morning
running over hillocks far and wide
just so we might reach the water's edge.

HARR RISING

Lapping waves in Spanish:
'olas rompiendo' as if
hellos could break open.

I study harr rising
from a line that
breaks sea // from sky

What is a horizon
if not unfirmly boundless:
in essence ephemerality?

I see sea, see waves
but the sound
does not exist

Silent movies, silent sea
silently, I turn my attention
to two strangers on the train.

Going from strangers to
the objects of this poem.
Warm light pours in on them

As they talk of homelands:
Canada, or Nova Scotia,
while breezing along the coast.

The harr has now risen
above that ceaseless water
full of boundary breaking: *Hello*.

GLOSSARY / GLOSARIO

Papá	[dad/daddy/but used for grandad in the poet's family]	avenidas	[avenues]
		leyenda	[legend]
		madre divina	[divine mother]
muñequita	[doll]		
bruja vieja	[old witch]	telenovela	[soap opera]
afuera	[outside]	música	[music]
primos	[cousins]	ritmo	[rhythm]
tus palabras	[your words]	protegerte	[protect you]
		mariposas	[butterflies]
lluvia	[rain]	crisálidas	[chrysalis]
lentamente	[slowly]	una promesa	[a promise]
hermoso	[beautiful]	calçada	[pavement; sidewalk]
querido	[darling]	olas rompiendo	[breaking waves]
mi alma	[my soul]		
mi rey	[my king]		
lo prometo	[I promise]		
cazadores	[hunters]		
mesa	[table]		
ofrenda	[offering]		
abuelo	[grandfather]		
pelo negro	[black hair]		
mi bisabuela	[my great grandmother]		
creciendo	[growing]		
burro	[ass/donkey/idiot]		

ACKNOWLEDGEMENTS

Previous versions of some poems have been published in the following places:

'Hurt' and 'Crescendo' – *All the Way Home* (Taproot Press, 2022)

'In praise of quiet boys' and 'A Man of Silences' – *Masculinity: An Anthology of Modern Voices* (Broken Sleep Books, 2024)

'Why I will not get out of bed' – Issue 8 of *Fourteen Poems Queer Poetry Anthology*

'The river turns into a waterfall' – *Re-creation: A Queer Poetry Anthology* (Stewed Rhubarb, 2021)

'In the Woods' – Issue 11 of *bath magg* (2023)

'In the name of the Joto, Mariposa y Maricón' – *Wasafiri* magazine (online) (2022)

'Memory Map' – *Wasafiri 117: The State of the Industry* (2024)

'Red, Red, Red' and 'If I could pray the gay away' – *He, She, They, Us: An Anthology of Queer Poems* (Pan Macmillan, 2024)

'An Echo Across Time' – an earlier version of this poem was commissioned as an audio poem for *Québec en toute lettres* in partnership with UNESCO Cities of Literature.

'Forty-one monarch butterflies dancing in a summer shower' is inspired by 'El Baile de los cuarenta y uno' which occurred in Mexico City on 17 November 1901. That evening the police raided a party in which forty-one men were in attendance, half of whom were dressed in women's clothes. Historically, it has been interpreted as a party of gay, queer, or 'sexually deviant' men and was illegal at the time. The group is sometimes referred to as '41 maricones' a derogatory term in Spanish for homosexual men. Marcicón and Mariposa are both used regularly as hate speech but like queer and faggot, have been reclaimed by many members of the gay and queer communities of Latin America.

'We shall gather' takes lines from '[Let Us Gather in a Flourishing Way]' by former US Poet Laureate, Juan Felipe Herrera.

'A Pile of Green Peas' takes inspiration from the painting *The Lustre Bowl with Green Peas* by Sir William Nicholson (1911) housed at The National Galleries of Scotland. In 2020, I was invited to write a short essay about the painting as the galleries prepared to open in Scotland after the first lockdown due to Covid-19.

Finally, some dedications: 'In the Woods' is for Marjorie Lotfi, 'When the wild calls' is for Hannah Lavery, 'Heron' is for Eris Young, and 'Good Friday' and 'Gay by definition' are for Edwin Morgan, a mentor I never met but who has influenced my writing like no other.

Finally, finally, some thank yous: I offer my deepest gratitude to Alycia Pirmohamed for her exceptional editing of this collection. These poems have been made braver, bolder and stronger by your wise and careful feedback. I would also like to thank Polygon, and especially Edward Crossan for taking a chance on this collection and my voice. You understood perfectly how I wanted to approach this next collection and for that I am utterly grateful.

Lastly, thank you dearest reader. A poet only becomes 'a poet' by virtue of someone deciding to read his poems! Big hugs and much respect.